Entrepreneurship Talk With A Real Boss

The Millennial Edition!

Learn business ins and outs from an accomplished serial entrepreneur of this generation. At the young age of 24, Jazmine Cheaves owns 3 different companies in 3 different industries and she is sharing all of her success secrets, business tips and strategies all in one book!

- Jazmine Cheaves -

TABLE OF CONTENTS

INTRODUCTION	10
LESSON 1: HOW TO START YOUR BUSINESS	13
LESSON 2: BRANDING & MARKETING STRATEGIES	27
LESSON 3: SETTING GOALS & DEADLINES	39
LESSON 4: BRAND IMAGE	44
LESSON 5: USING SOCIAL MEDIA PLATFORMS	50
LESSON 6: PROMOTIONS & ADVERTISING	54
LESSON 7: BUDGETING YOUR BUSINESS CAPITAL	57
LESSON 8: THE IMPORTANCE OF TAXES	62
LESSON 9: BUILDING A SUCCESSFUL TEAM	65
LESSON 10: ORGANIZING & STAYING CONNECTED WITH YOUR CUSTOMERS	71
ABOUT THE AUTHOR	81

© Copyright 2020 - All Rights Reserve

TERMS OF USE

This document is geared towards providing exact and reliable information in regards to the topic and issue covered. The publication is sold with the idea that the publisher is not required to render accounting, officially permitted, or otherwise, qualified services. If advice is necessary, legal or professional, a practiced individual in the profession should be ordered.

— From a Declaration of Principles which was accepted and approved equally by a Committee of the American Bar Association and a Committee of Publishers and Associations.

In no way is it legal to reproduce, duplicate, or transmit any part of this book in either electronic means or in printed format. Recording of this publication is strictly prohibited and any storage of this document is not allowed unless with written permission from the publisher. All rights reserved.

The information provided herein is stated to be truthful and consistent, in that any liability, in terms of inattention or otherwise, by any usage or abuse of any policies, processes, or directions contained within is the solitary and utter responsibility of the recipient reader. Under no circumstances will any legal responsibility or blame be held against the publisher for any reparation, damages, or monetary loss due to the information herein, either directly or indirectly.

Respective authors own all copyrights not held by the publisher.

The information herein is offered for informational purposes solely, and is universal as so. The presentation of the information is without contract or any type of guarantee assurance.

The trademarks that are used are without any consent, and the publication of the trademark is without permission or backing by the trademark owner. All trademarks and brands within this book are for clarifying purposes only and are owned by the owners themselves, not affiliated with this document or book.

DISCLAIMER

The author and publisher has strived to be as accurate and complete as possible in the creation of this book, notwithstanding the fact that she does not warrant or represent at any time that the contents within are accurate due to the rapidly changing nature of the internet. While all attempts have been made to verify information provided in this publication, the author and publisher assumes no responsibility for errors, omissions, or contrary interpretation of the subject matter herein. Any perceived slight on specific persons, peoples, or organizations are unintentional. In practical advice books, like anything else in life, there are no guarantees of results. Readers are cautioned to rely on their own judgment about their individual circumstances and act accordingly. This book is not intended for use as a source of legal, medical, business, accounting or financial advice. All readers are advised to seek services of competent professionals in the legal, medical, business, accounting, and finance fields.

DEDICATION

I dedicate this book to all my readers who are interested in learning more about entrepreneurship that took the necessary step to enhance your craft by purchasing my book :)

Congratulations on your journey to success. Hopefully my book plants a seed to a beautiful flower.

INTRODUCTION

Owning your own business can be a horrific thought for some, especially for people who know nothing about starting up their own business. The good news is that there are many resources available to help new entrepreneurs learn the ins and outs of company ownership. These resources include small business associations, seminars, and education degrees.

TALK TO OTHER ENTREPRENEURS

Learning from others who have taken the road you are interested in can be very useful. The important thing is to hear from a variety of people. Speaking with successful entrepreneurs can be inspiring. However, be sure to ask all of your questions and get feedback from entrepreneurs who have had both failures, as well as success.

ATTEND A SEMINAR, CONFERENCE, OR WORKSHOP

There are so many seminars, conferences, and workshops on entrepreneurship these days. These are great opportunities to learn some essential factors about business ownership in a short amount of time. Seminars and conferences can also be very encouraging because you are hearing from a motivated and successful speaker who usually shares tips to help you become successful as well.

VISIT A SMALL BUSINESS ASSOCIATION

Most cities and/or counties offer an SBA or a small business association where residents of the town who are interested in business ownership can go to get resources and tips on business and entrepreneurship. Some SBAs even offers office space for start-up entrepreneurs who are looking to get started with their business idea. SBAs offer seminars and workshops at little or no cost to people who are focused on entrepreneurship. They can walk you through the beginning process of starting your company and help guide you on the road to success within your geographic area.

EARN AN ENTREPRENEURSHIP DEGREE

Earning a degree with a focus on entrepreneurship is a definite way to get insight into what it takes to become a business owner. Many universities offer business degrees with a concentration on entrepreneurship and even have entrepreneurship centers to develop ideas and compete regionally and nationally with other aspiring entrepreneurs. Studying at a university almost guarantees that you will have someone who understands your passion for wanting to open your own business. You will be around other students who are interested in starting a company as well. This can be a very comfortable atmosphere where you are free to develop your business ideas and even have them challenged to make them better. University instructors engage students with entrepreneurial tasks and projects.

Overall, there are many ways to learn about starting your own business. A person may choose to learn about business ownership through one or all of the above methods. These are just some ways in which aspiring entrepreneurs can ask questions and have their questions answered by people who are considered to be experts in the area of entrepreneurship.

> "Scared money don't make no money."
>
> — JAZMINE CHEAVES

1 HOW TO START YOUR BUSINESS

If you are going to start your own business, you have to realize there will be bumps in the road. Naturally, everybody is making mistakes, and your performance can be determined by how well you handle those mistakes. However, you can avoid some things, so that you can get your business up and running as fast as possible. When you know what to watch out for, it's a lot easier to make money and help your customers. Here are some tips on how to start a business easily and effectively.

- First, you must consider what your company is about.

What is your niche?

Too many people rush into business with no ambitions, goals or plans. Don't be one of them. Take time to think about what business you think others could benefit from and where you could honestly see yourself being successful. When customers cannot trust your expertise, they will not want to buy what you sell or claim. Try something new, or with little competition. When you plans are more strategic, you can achieve even more.

- Identify your demographic.

When you have a marketing idea in mind, you need to decide who and where to market it.

There's always a population that profits more from what you've got to deliver. It's important to know these customers and how to reach out to them. Your strategy can be drawn from this. Conduct experiments if you have to so you can see how many people respond.

Who do you see on their pages the most often? Those are the people that you want to attract and understand fully.

- The bulk of all this is going to be in ads.

There are several different ways to market a brand, but relying on the audience is extremely effective for you. Go anywhere you want to go. If you know the people who use your company, services or product —request for feedback and use this information to get what they need. When you know that your audience is fond of socializing, go on some social networks. You can only know where to sell, but don't be afraid to explore several different ways to find something that fits you. Experimentation is supposed to bring your success.

START YOUR BUSINESS WITH THESE STEPS:

1. **OVERCOME YOUR FEARS:** Before you get started, you must give up on your fears. The fear of leaving your job, the fear of uncertainty, fear of failure, or anything that is stopping you from being successful. You have to understand that wealth is out there, waiting for you and you deserve to be happy, wealthy, and live the life of your dream.

2. **FIND A MENTOR:** Everyone needs someone to encourage them and point them in the right direction. It's a lot easier to model your business idea after someone already successful at what you are trying to do. Mentors can come from anywhere just make sure you are talking to the person looking out for your best interest. Don't forget that a good book can be a mentor too.

3. **SET GOALS:** You have to know where you are going. It's impossible to succeed at something if you don't see what you are trying to succeed in. It might seem like a simple step, but so many people don't get this right. Setting goals mean setting a defined outcome of what you are trying to accomplish and then setting smaller goals that lead to the primary goals.

4. **PLAN FOR SUCCESS:** Write out a plan of action. Not having a plan or strategy is just a plan waiting to fail.

Write out steps to your success. That is going to be your map to your goals, and it will also be a guide that will remind you of what you should be doing and keep you on your toes. A plan also keeps you from losing sight of why you are doing this in the first place. It also makes the steps real in your mind, giving you the fuel you need to get things done.

5. **EVALUATE YOUR STEPS:** Step back and take a look at what is going on with your business. Don't worry about making changes to your plans. Knowing where to spend your time, energy and resources is an essential part of running any business. You have to look at what's working and what's not. Think of Captain Kirk saying more power to the shields, at the critical time needed.

6. **TAKE ACTIONS:** Get started now! You have to take action. Don't just keep looking for the same answer over and over. Get step one out of the way. The best advice from the best people means nothing if you don't act on it!

HOW TO LEARN YOUR BUSINESS

Being a business owner, you are constantly searching for ways to expand your company. It is not uncommon for your thoughts to shift and grow when you begin to increase revenue and sense new opportunities but unplanned development can be just as dangerous as no growth at all for your business.

Fast growth can destabilize a company that gives its owners a false sense of security because the extra amounts of revenue can absorb more working capital than anticipated.

If you're aiming to expand your business, keep these things in mind.

WATCH YOUR OVERHEAD COSTS

The biggest danger in running a business and expanding is the loss of profit that comes from uncontrolled spending when you are just too busy to keep track of what is happening.

Overhead expenses under a controlled stabled business situation can overgrow to cover the extra costs associated with a bigger scale of operations - transportation, inventory, rental on larger storage space, and all the rest will eat in to your working capital levels if not managed correctly.

TRACK YOUR PROFIT MARGINS

You would generally expect to increase sale volumes and achieve the same profit margin, or even better since overheads will be spread across a more significant amount of sales income and because the cost of goods goes down as you buy in greater quantities.

Understand that this is not always the case.

Additional sales often come with unanticipated costs and reduced efficiencies that can decrease your margins. You need to regularly track your profit margins to see if you are growing or running faster to stay in the same place.

EMPLOY STRATEGICALLY

As you grow your business, it seems natural to hire more people.

A rapid hire of new workers will only cause issues ranging from shifting the dynamics of the old team, to creating moral problems, to increased costs of insurance, to benefits for employees.

Consider options such as retraining some of the current workers to take on new duties, taking on freelancers and resources, or even outsourcing some of the jobs or tasks needed.

Balance the time invested against the preparation investment they need and the skills you need to bring in to the business, and when they leave, these people will take their experience and abilities with them.

DON'T UNDERESTIMATE CASH FLOW REQUIREMENTS

A business organization is hungry for cash to fund higher levels of debt and inventory, and increased overheads and investment in capital.

Many small business owners may usually search for business

loans to expand operations. However, the risk here is that if the expansion does not go according to plans, the company will easily end up in the negative with a poor credit record.

Search for the cheapest and most reliable source of funds from approved suppliers, and provide a practical income and outflow forecast to understand the funding needs better.

KEEP CUSTOMERS LOYAL

Good customer service drives your business success, but ironically it is also one of the first things that tend to be forgotten when businesses go into expansion mode.

Employees can get caught up in the activity of the rapid business volume and lose track of what's happening to clients. Then the customer service that first helped you expand your company is hard to maintain, and customer defection occurs.

Securing new business can also be difficult to factor in to activities through the growth phase. Maintaining customers maintains sufficient staffing levels to ensure existing customers continue to receive the care and services that they have always been accustom to.

AVOID DISAGREEMENTS AMONG OWNERS

Multi-ownership can pose threats to the success of an expansionary drive.

Ownership arrangements that have functioned effectively before expansion activity can become increasingly problematic. As business challenges get more complicated, different owners' views on running the company and their vision of where it should go can diverge and lead to a conflict at the very top level.

When the expansion brings the management of operations beyond the capacity of one of the owners, the condition is especially difficult to deal with so that they no longer make a valuable contribution. If this occurs, the setting of a unified path for the company may allow one or more partners to leave.

You have to find a way to expand your company to thrive, and you shouldn't shy away from growing just because there are obstacles involved. Businesses are not struggling, but they are growing. We struggle because their managers do not control their growth or development. As per a sound business strategy, there is no substitute for expanding.

HOW TO GROW YOUR BUSINESS

I often hear business owners say, "What is the fastest way to grow my business?" There are so many things business owners can do to see an increase in gross revenue inexpensively (and immediately).

Most choices are simply an alternative "band-aid" but a few strategic changes from the inside out can truly transform any company. It's the kind of transformation that makes it so much easier for future marketing.

We all have limited time and resources, so try to make sure you're your business obtain the highest possible bang for it's buck for the same investment of time, emotion and money.

Question, where can a business owner invest their marketing time and energy to get the greatest impact?

What's an inexpensive yet powerful way to grow your business?

The one strategy that yields the highest return on investment is simply to take control of your marketing message.

This seems so basic and self-explanatory, but so many business owners miss this step and the negative results can cause marketing headaches for the business's life span.

Before we break down the steps of taking control of your marketing message, let's define what exactly is "marketing message."

A marketing message is the message or "point" you are communicating (or trying to communicate) in your business marketing, advertising, and sales. That message is the essence of who you are and what you are all about as a business.

All it takes is a discerning look at the advertising and marketing of a typical local business to identify that business' marketing message.

What most local business owners communicate in their "marketing message" is, "Hey, we're in the XYZ business (restaurant, dry cleaners, etc...), and here's our address!"

The message is nothing more than, "WE EXIST!"

If you don't believe me, pick up any local newspaper or magazine and look closely at the advertising. The typical ad identifies the type of industry/business and includes an address and a phone number... not much else.

The marketing message that such an ad conveys is, "We are 'a' restaurant, and there's nothing special that differentiates us from any other restaurant."

Nothing very exciting, engaging or memorable.

Ok, so we've defined marketing message. Now, how do you take control of it?

The two high impact steps to taking control of your marketing message are:

1. Creating a Unique Selling Proposition (USP)
2. Integrating that USP through out your marketing channels.

To take control of your marketing message:

- **STEP 1:** Determine Your Unique Selling Proposition (USP)

-The first approach in taking control of your marketing message is to explain precisely what makes your company different/unique for your target audience, and why they should do business with you (instead of doing business with your competitors).

-To skip this fundamental marketing step (as most local business owners do) is to leave it to your prospects and customers to define what your business is all about. They are left to categorize your business in any way they want, and their perceptions may or may not be based upon reality. Your marketing is now in their hands.

-In the minds of your target market, you'll likely remain "a" restaurant (or "a" dry cleaner, doctor, lawyer, etc...) ... instead of, "the only restaurant in the area that serves 100% organic foods, that has received the Governor's Award for Green cooking five years in a row, and that gives 10% of all profits to local organic farmers."

Do you see the difference? Now that's a message you can proudly communicate to the world! It's descriptive and memorable.

Do you see the danger of not taking control of this powerful and crucial step?

If your restaurant can brag about such things and don't find a way to incorporate those bragging points into your marketing message, you are leaving money on the table every day. I can guarantee you that your marketing is much less effective than it could (and should) be. You're leaving money on the table and flushing advertising/marketing dollars down the drain.

To begin the process of taking control of your marketing message:

- Figure out what makes your business unique, and provide a clear answer to why your customers should do business with you. The purpose is to identify your bragging points.
- Once you've done that, put those bragging points into a high impact statement of 90 words or less and be sure to make it memorable.

Now you've got a USP!

You've got the cornerstone of your marketing efforts.

You've set yourself apart from your competitors.

Now you're taking control of your marketing message and you are no longer giving away that power and control to others.

However, if you don't use your newly-created USP effectively, there's not much sense in having one.

That's why Step 2 is essential!

- **STEP 2:** Integrate Your Unique Selling Proposition into All of Your Marketing Channels

-This is where all of the hard work of step 1 pays off!

This is where you take full control of your marketing message and begin to see real results.

In Step 1, you created a high impact USP that articulates clearly what makes you unique and makes it clear to your customers why they should do business with you.

It's time to shout that message from the top of your lungs.

-Step 2 is to integrate and use that message in all of your marketing (business cards, banners/signs, websites, etc...) and advertising.

The goal is to constantly expose your target market to your marketing message (the message that you now control), prospects and customers need constant reminders.

It's time for you to take control!

-This one-two punch of taking control of your marketing message is inexpensive and very effective. It's the best place to start if you've got limited resources because it impacts every aspect of your marketing for the life span of your business.

It seems like something each and every business would naturally do. It only takes a glance at the advertising of most local businesses to see how rarely it's utilized.

So, what are you waiting for? You now know how to grow your business. Create your USP and start using it everywhere!

GROW YOUR BUSINESS THROUGH OUTSOURCING

If you are a business owner, you want to find ways to be able to expand your business.

People in business have the desire to expand their territories, and they have the willing heart to sacrifice their time and energy in to finding these means. However, your will alone is not enough to grow your business. You have to make use of creative strategies as well. In this competitive global market, you need to use proven strategies that can give you your desired outcome. One of the strategies that are being used by global businesses today is outsourcing.

For those who are not familiar with the term outsourcing, it is the method used to hire employees in a different area or country to do the work expected from regular staff. This means that the staff could be living in the Philippines while the company that he/she is working for is situated in the United States. Outsourcing is one of the answers to how to grow your business because it can help you save money by minimizing your power related expenses.

The key to how to grow your business is to minimize expenses and to increase production.

Outsourcing is one of the solutions to accomplish these goals. You can increase your production by getting the right employees for the job through outsourcing. When you put the right people to the right job, it will result in faster outcome with less wastage.

You can use outsourcing to help out existing teams when they need assistance in meeting deadlines and requirements. It is easy to hire people through outsourcing. You can establish a team easily. The best way to do this is to use outsourcing many platforms on the internet.

Outsourcing can truly help increase your productivity and efficiency. The best part about this is that you can do this while decreasing your power related costs and overhead costs. You can achieve this because outsourced employees can receive lower pay than regular employees. Outsourced employees don't expect fringe benefits as well. So, it means you have cut down costs already by hiring an outsourced employee.

Another thing is that an outsourced employee does not contribute to your company's expenses in terms of production costs. The outsourced employee is responsible for paying the expenses that he/she incurs while working on his/her assignment. Outsourcing is truly one of the best solutions on how to grow your business. You should learn more about it by visiting websites that has more in-depth information about this subject.

Do not limit yourself with an unaffordable workforce that you can only obtain locally. Outsource via a reliable platform, and you will see a bunch of skillful and talented professionals who are waiting to join your business empire.

If you know where to get these people online, you can save 50% more than normal local hiring. The saving of cost can be more than enough to help you in expanding the business.

HOW TO START A BUSINESS LEGALLY

The majority of the working population has and will always work for a "boss," simply because everyone else does, hence the "worker" mentality. The minority with entrepreneurial ideas, the dream is, and always will be, to come up with an idea to start a business and become rich from your efforts.

Based on this motivation, many businesses start, but simply because they are not familiar with the basics involved in running a business, they fail each year.

I will give you several suggestions you can use to ensure that your chances for success are greatly improved when starting your business. You need to be aware that there are certain risks to all business ventures. I do not accept any route being the only route or my ideas being the only valid way. On the contrary, I advise that you seek advice and assistance from a qualified accountant and solicitor before investing any money in a business venture. There will be times when their services will not be dispensable to you. Money spent on their fees may feel like a big and unnecessary expense, but they can help to avoid even bigger expenses, such as total or partial loss of your investment, or costly legal fees.

The first-ever thing that you should consider before starting or buying a business is the legal form under which you, your business, will be operating.

Four choices are available:

- Sole Ownership
- Partnership
- Limited Partnership
- Corporation

Each one has several advantages and disadvantages, so you have to decide which one is best for you.

An extremely simplistic view of your choices follows here. This is one time you should have a chat with an accountant to understand which will best suit you as it can get quite complicated.

1. As a sole proprietor or partner of a business, after all the expenses of running the business, you will pay taxes on your overall earnings, much the same as if you were in a paid or hourly job. If you're paying or not, getting the money out as a paycheck would have little effect on your company profits and tax return. You should be better

off than a salaried person because you can claim all the expenses. You are solely responsible for any debt you may occur from your business. Any property can be taken to pay any debts if you get into trouble.

2. As a partnership, all concerned parties are responsible for any liability or gain accrued to the business. The liabilities are just the same as the gain. You need to know your partners and trust them because you are liable for any debt that can occur. If the business causes a problem, you have to bear the entire cost of debt.

3. It is important to register a Limited Partnership, and it is equivalent to forming a new limited company. However, you can't purchase a limited liability partnership "off the shelf," as a limited company can. You will plan the original documents with the names of the first collection of "actual" partners.

4. If the business goes in to debt, a limited partnership helps you manage it without putting your private property at risk. But it does have a more complicated system of accounting.

Starting a business is a form of self-gratification for some people. They create a company just for the value of prestige just to say, "I am a company director." Please don't be this person. Make sure that purpose and passion is always the influence and motivation behind your business, or anything you do in life with good intentions.

HOW TO START A BUSINESS

Prospective business owners looking to learn how to start a business will find a number of resources and information online. It's important to become familiar with the necessary and suggested steps of creating a business, filing all appropriate documentation, and commencing the legal, ongoing creation of that business.

- First, there are several great, official guides that you can use online to help you get started and learn more about how to start a business per state. These are great choices to help you learn how to start a business in your state.

Of course, neither replaces real legal assistance and consultation. This will be a crucial step to ensure that all of your documents and registrations are filed properly, all of the required measures are taken, and that your business plan complies with any local or state laws and regulations.

Nonetheless, as mentioned, online is a great place to begin.

See list of 8 steps, each one of which is broken down further into specific tasks or goals.

In order, they are as follows:
- The business plan
- Counseling and advice
- Choose a location.
- Legal structure.
- Select a business name.
- Access to capital
- Registration.
- State and local licenses and permits.

Here's a great overview on how to start a small business and it also provides additional resources to continue learning, as well as more information about each step. Of course, it's crucial to remember that no businesses are alike and everyone has unique needs.

> Dont expect support.
> You are the support!

JAZMINE CHEAVES

2 BRANDING & MARKETING STRATEGIES

You own a small business, and you're doing well, but recently you have noticed that your competitors have a slight edge. Wondering why? Chances are, it has nothing to do with your product or price - it's the simple fact that they are more memorable than you.

There are two ways that you can increase your memorability.
- The first is through advertising and marketing
- The second is through small business branding and brand strategy.

To learn more, continue reading this piece. In this chapter, we will discuss the branding basics and give you some need-to-know branding tips.

Before we discuss branding tips, let's begin by discussing a simple question: what is branding?

Think about small business branding as a definition of what the clients think your business is about. With a good brand strategy, you can easily differentiate your services or products from those of your competitors, giving you the leading edge. To clarify, let's use a brief example.

You wake up late one morning, and if you don't leave soon, you will be late for work. You don't have time to make your breakfast, but you do have time to stop for a quick drive through for a bite. As you think about where to go, you suddenly hear "Badabababa, I'm lovin it" play in your mind. Where do you head? Towards the golden arches!

Why did you choose McDonald's?

You may think that it is because their food tastes great (and that can be part of it), but doesn't most fast food taste good?

Most people do not realize that many of the decisions they make are based on branding.

McDonald's has developed a great tag line that sticks in our heads. On top of that, anyone over the age of 3 knows what the golden arches represent. Small business branding, or a good tagline and a memorable logo, plays a significant role in McDonald's success in the past decades.

By creating a strong brand strategy and developing your tagline and logo, you can also see your business expand by making it memorable to your clients.

Let's cover some cool branding tips to help you build a magnetic brand.

First of all, there are many things that you can do to increase the success of your logo and tagline. However, of all the branding tips available, there is one that stands out as the most important: small business branding alone is not enough. Once you have developed a brand strategy, logo, and tagline, you must follow through on your promises. If your tagline is "I'm lovin it," you better keep customers loving it. You can do this through brand management.

Brand management involves many things, each of which is designed to keep your customers happy and keep them remembering your brand in a positive light. Brand management can include manufacturing a high-quality product, keeping your prices reasonable, and providing high-quality customer service.

When you own a company, small businesses' branding will become a required part of attracting clients. You will be making your business memorable by developing a brand for your customers, keeping them interested and most importantly, returning.

When there is one piece of information you should take away from the branding tips, it is this one: it is not enough to brand alone. You also need to engage in tactics of brand management to ensure that your brand is positive, rather than negative. Start developing a brand strategy for your business and give something to remind your customers of.

BUSINESS BRANDING FOR SUCCESS

The one thing you need to have is branding that is compatible with your company and your true self if you want to be successful.

Branding separates you from your competitors and gives you a reputation. That's what makes people want to spend and buy from you.

Without branding, companies will not thrive.

Your eyesight is greater than your ability. Visibility counts. To increase your exposure, branding is essential for the recognition of your company. People need to know who you are as they're more likely to buy from you and recommend you to others.

See below, and you can strive for emphasis on the brand and advocacy.

- Brand awareness: they know your name.
- Brand preference: they prefer to use you.
- Brand insistence: they buy only your product or service.
- Brand advocacy: they tell other people about you.

Use something memorable to develop a strong logo and slogan for your business, so that people will remember the name.

Control of your mark is important. A lack of brand control while driving is like having no one at the steering wheel and trying to figure out how to control it.

- Your brand is exactly what the first impression people have of you.
- You must strive to be consistent.
- Make anything you come in line with, consistent.
- Consistency makes loyal customers.

Points you need to consider when branding:
- Profitability: will it help you become profitable?

- Marketability: is it something you can market?
- Credibility: is it credible?
- Visibility: how will you make it visible?
- Invisibility: you need to ensure you stand out and you are not invisible
- Instability: invokes stability?

Regarding brand recognition in the long term, consider the following:

- The money needed to get yourself branded?
- How to get yourself branded?
- What to brand?
- Is that consistent with your company and yourself?
- Can you relate to that when you look through a mirror?

Feedback Similar to:

- Social branding (remember, this is your branding).
- Brand association (brand your business, so your branding fits in).
- Product Innovation (is it separate from innovation?).
- Brand reputation (is that real, or is it a good outlook?).
- Any time a customer buys or invests in you, you've got a good branding.
- Branding is something of creative art.
- Branding includes presentation, persuasion, sales, and negotiation.
- Analyzing the desire of your prospective customer to buy is key to building your brand.
- Control message branding; make sure you control the message that you are sending out.
- People will buy from you for these reasons:

- They have an issue that you have a solution for.
- They have a problem or need, but they're not sure if it can be solved.
- You told them you were the authority and not just the expert.
- Individuals feel no need for your product or service, but you've persuaded them that they need it.
- Customers would buy from you to relieve unhappiness with some other goods or services.
- You are selling your product or service against what they already have; it's brand positioning.
- You conquer their fear of change and encourage them to leave their comfort zone; your brand gives them peace of mind.
- As a natural extension of their lives, you mark yourself as a complement rather than a destructive transition.

Top 2 Basic Rules In Business:

a. The customer is always right.

b. When in doubt, refer back to number 1.

THERE IS A DIFFERENCE BETWEEN NEEDS AND WANTS

Here are 5 fundamental factors that prevent people from being successful in business. This can be solved by a branded person, product, or service.

- Fear
- Procrastination or lack of focus
- Lack of education
- Time management
- Accountability

Successful businesses think about what they can do for the

consumer, and the typical company talks about what they can do for the customer. Brand to the formula of WIFM, and take care of "so what."

People are more likely to buy the brand than the product. Your reputation is directly related to your brand, including branded handbags, suits, shoes, coffee shops, restaurants, etc.

Customers do business with you not because you get the best deal, but because they trust you and respect you. This you can not afford to buy. People are not buying auto insurance, which they are paying. Branding lends a sense of security to people.

Understanding the primary and sub-influences is important.

- First: Why they buy without thought.
- Secondary: there are explanations and excuses that people rationalize why they shouldn't buy.

All decisions regarding transactions are subjective, seldom rational. Logically people will invest but buy emotionally. To suit this, the branding needs to set the framework.

You need to grasp decision-making on the left and the right side. Left brains think rationally, numbers while the right brain person thinks artistically and creatively (45% left brain, 45% right brain and 10% both) Build your brand, so it appeals both left and right brain people. Your key to success will be this.

Find the emotional red button to get people to purchase your product or service and build your brand. The perfect place to do that is to create surveys to question your prospective customer specifically.

- Ways to brand yourself
- Achievement
- Association
- Authoring a book
- Reciprocation
- Third-party recognition
- Charitable donation

ALWAYS UNDER PROMISE AND OVER DELIVER

Then start connecting all elements of your business and any other company you have to that brand. All over your business, there should be congruence, so everything else is related to everything else.

In other words, your signage, websites, paperwork, business cards, and everything in your business should reflect your logo and slogan and have the same colors and text, making them uniform. They'll know you. Using your name is NOT best.

Appearance is indeed a key element; depending on the type of business you are in, and the type of image you want to represent, you should dress. Keep in mind that your look represents your business, so dress appropriately, in line with your company.

Use Hotmail, Gmail, and other similar generic email addresses do not offer your business status, use email addresses specific to your business, preferably the same email address as your website. Remember that first names in email addresses appear to signify a small business before using the first name for the email addresses. If you want to look like a big corporation, then you need to use something more formal.

It's not easy to do, but if you master it, your business will become successful and recognized.

MARKETING STRATEGIES

Most small to medium-sized companies are faced with a difficult fight, a juggling act of plans, policies, divisions, and decisions. All the elements are present, all the gears are in working order, but business is not exactly booming to the speed it had expected or projected. What exactly does it take for growth and sustainability? This is about standing out from the crowd in a tumultuous world teeming with congested airwaves and violent market practices. And interestingly, this has a lot more to do with your marketing campaign than you would expect.

By implementing a brilliant marketing plan, not by shouting louder than their rivals or putting neon banners on their storefront (or banner advertising on their website), impacted business owners can conquer the mazes and attract consumers right for their product. My point is that you don't just have to put yourself out there with a lot of noise. What you need to do is paint a vision for your business, your employees, and your clients. Make promises you can keep no one but you, and then blow them away with your impressive corporate practices and supernatural abilities.

Taking a moment to ponder this: Advertising campaign is the most significant factor in assessing a business's success or decline. That's a pretty significant assertion, and I'm prepared to prove its validity. Marketing strategy distributes itself through all aspects of a company, whether its founder wants to or not. It is possible because the plan is developed and defined by a particular business's overall objectives and combines those objectives with the company's unique vision and purpose. Simply put, the marketing strategy should be oozing on every level of a company. Verily!

Does that sound far-fetched? Let's look at the marketing strategy relationship and the four key aspects of any business: market research, marketing plan, corporate identity, and economy. First, let's get out of the formalities and give a definitive explanation of what marketing strategy is. I have decided on a less-official but more accurate summary of marketing strategy after scouring many websites for the official concept.

It is a strategy that integrates the marketing goals of an organization into a cohesive whole. Ideally drawn from market analysis, it focuses on the optimal combination of goods to achieve the optimum potential for profit. A Marketing Strategy lays out the marketing plan.

Although your marketing plan is simply a text, it has a much more load-bearing nature. The plan will include your mission statement and company goals, an exhaustive list of your goods and services, a summary or overview of your target markets, and a specific definition of how you fit into your industry's competitive environment.

MARKETING STRATEGY VS. MARKET RESEARCH

The relationship establishes an order of operations. Research is the first step of any advertisement or branding project. Whether it's a broad overview of your current customer base or revealing specific, detailed results from your target market, the result will have a direct impact on your marketing strategy, regardless of the scope of your study. It's imperative to find out all you're trying to reach about. In which age is it in? How big is their family? Where are they living, eating, and hanging out? Where should they spend their money and free time? Each of these information will affect your marketing plan and will change it.

Research alone without a solid marketing strategy won't benefit your company. The collection and organization of data for business purposes is often narrowly defined by business owners as market research. And while this is theoretically a precise definition, the emphasis is not on the research process itself. Now, the effect it enjoys on a company's future decisions affecting all rates. - the business decision presents unique information needs, and this information then shapes a marketing strategy that is appropriate and applicable.

Analysis can be a grueling, boring, and confusing process. From setting up or cleaning up a database to creating surveys and conducting interviews, you can get lots of information about your customers and potential customers, and wonder what to do next. The information and the data collected must be structured, processed, analyzed, and stored before beginning to formulate a strategy. Rest assured, this will all be transformed into an organized, efficient, and easily adaptable marketing strategy with a little imagination and lots of effort. Besides, ongoing and updated research will ensure the approach is an up-to-date and appropriate representation of your target market, marketing priorities, and future business activities.

MARKETING STRATEGY VS. MARKETING PLAN

The marketing strategy in this partnership is a guide for assessing a specific marketing campaign's success and efficacy. Simply put, a marketing strategy is a description of what you are selling and how you are positioning yourself in the market (in comparison to the goods and services of competitors), and your marketing plan is a structured list of steps that you will execute to achieve the goals outlined in your strategy. The plan would cover the steps toward a real-world implementation of a marketing strategy, bringing your mission and vision to the world. It's your time to demonstrate and sell your goods and services and encourage your target audience and experience them the way you imagined them.

Businesses also lack a combination between personality creativeness and personality logic. In contrast, a business owner may have the imagination to dream up a brilliant product, business model, and brand, study, preparation, and execution that lack the ambition and discipline to bring it all to life.

MARKETING STRATEGY VS. CORPORATE IDENTITY

It's no wonder that some of the world's most popular and recognizable businesses are the ones who build exclusive, one-of-a-kind cultures that permeate every aspect of a company and touch consumers on a human level. A corporation's culture, psychology, attitude, business approaches, values, and beliefs lay the foundations for a unique and compelling corporate identity. There's a strong and undeniable connection between these companies' health and the identities their culture has provided.

The delicate balance between a brand and a strategy has been discovered by these companies and how this symbiotic connection encourages visibility and growth. The relationship is simple: the marketing plan reflects where an organization wants to go, and the community dictates how it is going to get there (and often whether). Only ask of a brand identity Style, words, pictures, and colors-to personify your marketing strategy. In every phase of the marketing strategy, the corporate identity is extended and applied and plays a stylistic role in its execution.

MARKETING STRATEGY VS. THE ECONOMY

The economy is an extremely important subject around the world. We've also noticed that many companies and business owners use a depressed economic state as a reason (and, in some cases, an excuse) for their business deficiencies.

For example, layoffs have been a big trend recently. Larger companies use poor economies to kill their workers and slash jobs when they realize just as well that it is the very opposite of what needs to happen, or does it happen? It's getting hard to say. Is it so easy to endure a "depression" as, say, to reassess your marketing strategy? Although an unstable economy is troubling, risky, and unpredictable, it's also an excellent indicator of the marketing strategy 's flexibility. You don't set your strategy in stone ... Firstly, creating a plan is to maneuver smoothly through any given situation, be it good or bad. Unfortunately, many CEOs and CFOs first target their marketing departments in lean times. The fact is that they will invest in these areas so that their marketing managers can change their strategies to live during difficult times, or even prosper.

Most businesses view marketing as a discretionary cost, making it a simple budget cutter target. It's like marketing is a luxury that's only afforded when times are flush. Less demand from the customers, less marketing we can afford, or so conventional thinking goes. But can we ever afford not marketing?

Wanting to keep the cash during a downturn is natural. I've been an employer for almost fourteen years, so I feel sympathetic. But when sales go south, the tendency is to make deep cuts in marketing. Companies also begin to reduce or remove external costs, such as advertisements, conferences, sponsorships, studies. And they lay off workers in the marketing industry, even the whole department when that's not enough.

The net result of declining marketing is to stifle growth, profitability, and customer interest retention when these issues are most important. It's a penny-wise, dumb decision.

YOUR MARKETING STRATEGY

Although marketing strategy is not measurable, it is as dear to its place in business as the product or service. Its contribution bears significance through every phase of a business plan, from conception to execution and far beyond the aspects of research, planning, identity, and economy.

The marketing strategy will continue to fold into the company plans as long as it is correctly developed and executed. Research on your industry and competitors will allow you to establish a proper, versatile strategy and formulate it. The marketing plan serves as a blueprint to bring the strategy to life, meet and attain the defined goals, while developing your corporate culture and identity at the same time. Know, this piece of culture works in two ways. Your culture helps shape the approach, and then the culture will be improved. Ultimately, the approach needs to be both solid and versatile enough to endure the most challenging or unpredictable conditions in the industry, such as economic crisis, emerging developments, or competitions.

The strategy is a tiny piece of a much larger picture. At times anything can be daunting. Yeah, but the fun is part of that. The pieces will come together with ease with determination, preparation, and a champion marketing team, allowing the awesome personality of your company to shine out and profits to follow quickly.

3 SETTING GOALS & DEADLINES

When a new year starts, many people make promises for the upcoming year to do something special. Sadly, within a few weeks, almost 60 percent of these resolutions will be broken by the middle of the year. While the resolutions of the new year set out the intent to change, they are not enough. A commitment to a new year is a good first step. It is a declaration of your intention to change. Often, it declares the result that you want to have.

The argument itself is not typically strong enough to make the change happen. All you need is a GOAL.

Goals vary from resolutions because there are necessary steps to allow you to reach the goal. One target requires action from you. It is a wish, without consequence. You may want to lose weight or get out of debt, for example, but the idea alone isn't enough to happen without a plan and some action.

The start of a new year can be a great time to set new targets for the months ahead. I usually suggest people set goals that can be accomplished in a few months, with the longest being six months. I think something longer than that can be a struggle to keep the momentum going. If you have something big and long-term that you want to accomplish, set goals along the way, such as a new career or writing a book, you will have to be able to keep alive your faith alive to reach your target.

TOP 3 STEPS TO SETTING YOUR GOAL

1. **Find out what you want.**
It might sound obvious, but you'd be shocked how many people concentrate on what they don't want instead. For example, you might not want to be in debt, you may not want to be overweight or you may not want to be so stressed out. All of these are goals you don't want to achieve. The real question here is; what do you want? The clearer that you can be on this, the better.

2. **State the purpose as a target for S.M.A.R.T.**
A S.M.A.R.T. target involves fulfilling the words described in the acronym, SMART, by letters as your goal should ALWAYS be clear.

STRATEGY: (S in S.M.A.R.T.)
- The more precise the target is, the more you're going to focus in on exactly what you want.

For starters, if you aim to have more money, you'll have to find out just how much more. If you're just setting your target to have "more," are you going to be happy if you just earn one more dollar?

Choose a single dollar amount you'd like to have. If you want to lose weight by the same token, figure out what you want to weigh and be clear about it.

MEASURABLE: (M in S.MA.R.T.)
- Be sure to find out how your performance can be calculated. Make observable your goal.

This gives you the ability to learn when you hit it. If your goal is to lose weight, how much weight would you like to lose? Without understanding this, you will not know whether or not you have managed to achieve the goal.

AFFIRMATIONS: (A in S.M.A.R.T.)
- When selecting your target, state it as if it is happening right now.

For example, "I put 10 percent of my income aside into savings every month," or "I eat four servings of fruits and vegetables every day." By mentioning your target as if it had already been accomplished, you establish it in your mind as a fact. It's happened before. For the future, it is not something that you delay until "someday." You rush, instinctively, to make it happen.

REALITY: (R in S.M.A.R.T.)
- Your goal must be practical.

The objective must be achievable. For example, if I set a goal by the end of the week to earn a million dollars, that is probably not realistic. If I set a goal for the day after tomorrow to lose 20 pounds, it can not be done healthily. Those are not realistic goals. Pick something realistic for you, and a practical deadline too.

TIMING: (T in S.M.A.R.T.)
- Targets need a deadline.

You must set a deadline for their accomplishment when you set a target. Otherwise, there's no impetus, no urgency to reach it. The timetable stops it from being just a "someday" wish. Once you set a deadline for your goal, you put yourself on a path to start working on it and draw on some motivation to continue working towards it.

3. **Write down the requirements.**
Objective S.M.A.R.T.

It gets rooted in your mind by writing it down as something you will achieve.

Following these three simple steps in your goal setting for your business will automatically sett yourself up to achieving success.

THINGS TO REMEMBER WHEN SETTING GOALS

Set realistic goals and have a straightforward plan to meet them before you set out to.

1. **SET GOALS THAT MATTER**

Setting goals that result in you becoming a happier person, becoming able to perform a job better, or just enhancing your life PERIOD- are all good things. However, when you find yourself interested in certain things, make sure it matters to you.

There are several different ways you can pretend to be a boss, so don't waste your time pretending to be someone you're not. The results MUST be big for you to accomplish something meaningful. It must lead to a better way of living and loving life or you'll miss the important logic behind the goal if you don't have a goal that counts. You must have the inspiration, motivation, integrity, values, and passion because if your heart's not in it from the jump, your business will not flourish.

2. **THE TIME FRAME**

You need to have a time frame when setting a goal to achieve the goal.

For example, if all of your debts need to be paid off, you may need to give yourself some time to get there. If your trying to lose weight, you might want to give yourself a few months. My point is, there has to be a time frame in every event because if you don't set a time limit for yourself, there will be no deadlines.

Here are a few questions to ask while considering deadlines:

- How much time do I need to commit to that goal every day?

If you can't spend much time on it, don't expect to achieve it in a shorter amount of time.

- Why do I need a goal?

If you need the incentives to get that target right away, you might need to set your deadline closer.

- Is the goal small or big?

If a goal is small, it can be accomplished within a short timeframe. The bigger the goal is, the more time it takes to achieve.

Asking the right questions will make sure that the timeline you give yourself is correct.

3. **GOAL SPECIFICS**

The more focused you are on your goal, the more you can achieve it. It's easy to say, "I want to lose weight", but when you insert the goal and say: "I want to lose 30 pounds in 4 months." It's a lot easier to track your progress. You will also need to have weekly goals and routines to help you achieve the ultimate goal.

A clear goal carries a potential strategy with it. You should make the milestones that you have to achieve along the way. Now that you have the map, all you have to do is get in the car and drive to your destination.

4. **BE REALISTIC**

Set goals that make sense.

Of course I want you all to be enthusiastic about reaching your goals to greater things, but please understand that in order to be great, you must be decent first. You just can't skip this step. Make sure you make the high school varsity team before you head out to play in the NBA.

Here are some common areas where people fail to achieve their realistic targets:

- Making money:

Everyone wants to get to the big bucks immediately, but don't want to make the necessary steps or sacrifice with the hard work your business may need in order to flourish immediately.

- Health:

Your body is so important. The last thing you want to do is push yourself to hard to where you're not able to run your business. Mental health is just as important as physical health and you need both to operate efficiently as well as professionally. Before you plan to be the best athlete in any sport, give yourself enough time to understand your body!

- Knowledge:

In a short amount of time, you really can't learn anything. Every day you must be willing to learn and work a little at making your business better. Information is the key and training or learning more about your business will only unlock your business success and make it stronger.

5. **CHALLENGING GOALS**

Challenge yourself to something worth achieving. Make it to where you will need to change certain behaviors, attitudes, or thoughts that will stay with you forever for you to get it. Achieving a truly challenging goal comes with a great feeling of victory that most other endeavors don't match. You end up being better than before and the goal not only tested your mind but also tested your body, your spirit, your soul.

4 BRAND IMAGE

Branding, creating, and maintaining your image can be a powerful tool in helping you become the type of professional that you want to be. Why would someone want to brand themselves you ask?

Think about this in the way you'd think about getting any product on the market. If you were to market a new car, you could be talking about the car's features, such as gas mileage or how safe it is. Also, you'd find out who you're going to sell this car too. You wouldn't want to sell a two-door sports car to a large family of six. Now would you? When you market a car, you'll want to tell customers the promises and guarantees that separate them from others. The marketing style is very similar to your brand.

Keep in mind you also have to sell yourself to your future managers and employers by highlighting your features and company mission.

You also need to know who you're trying to target with your company, your brand message, and what you're hoping to achieve in your work. You will build a strong professional brand identity by promoting yourself as a unique person, understanding your target audience, as well as creating and maintaining your brand message and promise. To further develop your image, it is important to know who you are, and your existing personal brand. I want you to think about questions like- what makes you who you are. What makes you different from the rest? You can start moving your brand forward by staying true to yourself first. Think of your personal beliefs and what kind of person you are. Those are the things that make you who you are. Do not try to change who you are or want your image to be. If you change and adapt to who you want to create an image of or for, you 're not creating a personal brand image. You 're creating a generic brand image that doesn't emphasize what you're offering on a specific level. The brand identity needs to expand from what you already have. Reflect on what makes you who you are and create a professional brand identity based on certain qualities that currently exist.

When you've established this current personal brand, you can start looking at how you can make your brand special, set yourself apart, and develop your unique brand identity. What do you deliver as a specialist, for example, and what do you bring to others? These are the characteristics that set you apart from the competition. These are the things that will make you stand out from others around you and create a positive brand image. The first steps toward developing your own unique and specific personal brand are a positive attitude and confidence in your abilities, and what you know you can achieve.

It's important to develop skills, along with your attributes, that will set you apart from others around you. Reflect on what you are going to do to go above and beyond all the other brands. It will help you build your brand identity, which will take potential clients from wanting the services and expertise they know you are providing from potentially wanting your services for themselves as an actual customer or client. Focusing on strong communication skills with your potential clients is also important. This can be a positive step towards boosting your brand by building a strong relationship between you and your customers. It also helps you maintain a healthy client/customer relationship.

Your exclusive personal brand identity will set you apart from the competition and help you create lifelong customer relationships. Understanding n what your brand message will be and what guarantees you can make while building your brand identity is so important. You have to set the brand values in place. These principles are the resources that you can add to any and every situation, even at the workplace. Your message MUST focus on what you are specializing in as you're distinguished by your unique brand image attributes and leadership skills. This brand message will allow your potential customers to see who you are and to understand what you, your services and work will provide. Clients also need to be able to see what the promise of your brands is to them. Your brand promise should focus on your service commitment, what you can accomplish for the potential customer, and, finally, your reputation. It's important to tell customers that you might not be perfect. Using this as a form of communication to the clients, ensures them that the problem has been handled, learned from, and will not be repeated in the future if errors have been made in the past.

You are taking the most important steps toward success by building your brand identity. Look at who you are, knowledge your accomplishments and how far you've become and concentrate on your special skills. Be sure to always differentiate yourself from the competition around you, and sustain your reputation by service dedication. You can build and keep a positive brand identity through these measures to contribute to your brand advantages and performance.

IMPROVING THE BRAND IMAGE OF YOUR BUSINESS

Brand image is a very important factor within your business and it is something you definitely need to concentrate on. With a good brand image, you can bet on that you will have and keep loyal customers, which means you'll always have certain revenue. You now can set your prices higher because the brand image means that people will still be willing to buy your products. With a good brand image, people see you are a more than a trustworthy business, which promotes more sales and revenue, which eventually converts to good profit and sales volume.

Here's a list of three things I put together for you of the best ways to boost your brand identity. These tips will not only help you to improve your brand image, but they will definately help you increase your business audience, leading to more sales and interests.

1. **IMPROVE THE QUALITY OF YOUR PRODUCT OR SERVICE**

One of the easiest ways to boost your brand identity is by offering something of high quality to your customers. By having a quality brand, you can ensure that you have that edge over your competitors. You can also make sure that you have the potential of charging a higher price, which would lead to a greater profit margin.

The main reason for doing this is so that you build up a customer base who buys your product or services because of what you are offering, not because of the price. People are more likely to buy something if they know it will last and get the most out of it.

A problem of improving quality is that it will lead to increased costs in the short-term. I still believe it is a very important operation to carry out because, in the long-term, it will sustain and distinguish your company while keeping people coming back to you.

2. IMPROVE YOUR LOCATION AND PLACING

This may sound weird crazy but the location is a very important factor when trying to set up and improve your brand image. Please believe me when I say that people will see location as a factor in whether they will use your brand or not. For example, people who live in hood or projects have a different lifestyle than people who live in a country estate. This of course is all in my personal opinion, but you will need to identify your location depending on who your targeted demographic is.

So why does location affect your brand image?

Convenience. The easier you are to get to, or the easier it is to contact you, buy from you, whatever, depending on what you do, will affect your brand image. People want to be able to buy your product or use your service easily, without too much trouble. The better placed you are, the more likely people will come looking for you. The irony of this is that the better brand image you have, the more likely people will spend time finding you.

The location also means where your product is placed in shops, or where your advertisements are—all of these need to be in the right places to appeal to your targeted audience.

3. USE PROMOTION TO YOUR ADVANTAGE

I made this last because the other two can affect it a lot. If you have a good quality product, promotion may not be needed as people will promote it for you. There is nothing wrong with letting people spread the word for you as word of mouth is the fastest way to get the word out! Location can also promote everything for you. If you have your product in the right place, in a shop, etc... people will see it. If you have your office in the correct location, people will see it, taking away the need for promotion.

However, promotion can help improve your brand image tremendously. This is because you can make people believe things about your company (hopefully they will be true!). With promotion and marketing, you can tell people why you are a great business, why you deserve customers, and what you will and can do for them. Promotion is a great tool to get across what you want to get across, and this makes it the most important aspect of building a brand image. Even with a poor-quality product and poor location, you can still get a great brand image from amazing promotion. Promotion for a business is key.

From the above 3 points, I have tried to give some insights into how to improve your business's brand image. They are in no order, but please understand that the last one is the most important! This is because, as explained above, promotion can change everything. The other two are important, but they don't make so much of a difference than what could be achieved with a bomb promotions. Your brand image can make or break your company. So, make sure you keep every eye on it.

> I started winning when I started betting on myself.
>
> — JAZMINE CHEAVES

5 USING SOCIAL MEDIA PLATFORMS

One of the most expensive mistakes to make as a business owner is to say that social media is a waste of time. Skipping social marketing because you're just "not with" will leave you missing countless opportunities to build your brand, spread your message, expand your reach, and boost your sales. All businesses are now using a free marketing tool from national to local companies. Please don't leave them behind. These are the top reasons you could end up failing or falling behind.

MOST COST-EFFECTIVE WAY WITH THE INTERNET

Why spend so much money on online advertising tactics such as Banner Ads, or Pay Per Click when you can access millions of potential customers for free via social media sites? All free social media sites you can join from Instagram, Facebook and Pinterest.

REACH PEOPLE FROM THE OTHER SIDE OF THE WORLD

That is internet elegance. To get your message across, you don't need to fly to other nations when you can simply do it in seconds , right in front of your computer screen. People around the globe use social media sites, particularly famous ones like Instagram, TikTok and Facebook. These marketing platforms give you global scope without the need to spend too much money.

GET IN TOUCH WITH YOUR TARGET MARKET AND DEMOGRAPHICS

Since marketing is all about touching base with your target audience, you can take advantage of social media features to achieve this goal. Social sites definately offers you a chance to join communities with common ambitions and interests. For example, if you're a graphic design company, you can join a community of graphic designers on Facebook. That puts you in a better place to find yourself online.

FIND STAFF, INFLUENCERS AND AFFILIATES

Social networks don't just bind you to potential clients. They also pave the way to get to know other people, including staff, potential buyers, partners, and sponsors, who can be an asset and support your company in a different way.

To begin with, those are only four good reasons. Certain factors for using social media include: enhancing customer or consumer interaction and engagement, performing market research, building brand awareness, gaining authority, knowledge and credibility, increasing traffic to the website, tracking popularity, creating more leads, learning more about competition, seeking referrals, and so much more.

ADVANTAGES OF SOCIAL MEDIA FOR YOUR BUSINESS

Social media is better understood as a collection of emerging online media styles that share all of the functions below. It invites all interested parties to help and to provide feedback. Many social media services are open to feedback and interaction. They promote voting, feedback, and information-sharing. There are unusual obstacles to user access and use (password-protected user is frowned upon).

There are six social media types currently.

1. **SOCIAL SERVICES**

These sites allow individuals to create personal web pages and to communicate with friends to share content and communication. Facebook, Twitter, Instagram, etc ... are the biggest social networks.

2. **BLOGS**
The best-known type of social media, blogs are online newspapers, with entries with the most recent current events or gossip.

3. **INFORMATIONAL RESOURCE**
These websites enable individuals to add or edit material to the information on them, serving as a common document or database. The best-known wiki is Wikipedia, the online encyclopedia featuring more than 2 million articles in English.

4. **PODCASTS**
Audio and video files are available by subscription through services such as Apple iTunes.

5. **QUESTIONS**
Online discussion areas, often around particular topics and interests. Forums existed before the word "social media" and are a strong and common part of online culture.

6. **CONTENT COMMUNITIES**
The groups are communicating and sharing various content styles. The most popular content categories tend to be the photographs (Flickr), bookmarked links (del.icio.us), and videos (Youtube).

7. **MICROBLOGGING**
Social networking in conjunction with bite-sized blogging, where small quantities of content ('updates') are transmitted online and over the mobile phone network. Twitter is the obvious leader in this area.

HOW DOES SOCIAL MEDIA MARKETING HELP YOU TO GROW YOUR BUSINESS?

Social media marketing has revolutionized the marketing cycle in a major way. Because of it's technical origin, the strategies are more common and are based on social networks like Instagram, Twitter, TikTok, Linkedin and Facebook.

The strategy is gaining popularity. Social media marketing is one marketing methodology that has proven its worth to the fullest in the most difficult economic times.

You will hit the top by using various on-line marketing strategies that will create a lot of traffic and help your company in the long term. This can help you expand to more traffic and leads, get an immediate response, improve immediate sales, create loyal customers, and calculate investment returns as well.

As a consequence of the direct or indirect influence of social media advertisers, consumers today are more likely to make decisions based on what they read and see in channels that we call "social," but only if they are informed by someone they have learn to trust. This is why a purposeful and carefully planned social media strategy has become an important part of every marketing campaign.

6 PROMOTIONS & ADVERTISING

In the world of business, whenever the term "promotions" is spoken, people immediately think that it is about media advertising. While there is some truth to this, it's more to it. Media advertising is facing a stiff challenge from another marketing method, which is Promotional Advertising.

WHAT IS PROMOTIONAL ADVERTISING?

People associate promotions with the media. Media advertisement can be very costly and does not always deliver, therefore different methods are required. This is where promotional advertisement comes into place. This is a type of promotion where promotional companies take a leading role and approach. Many companies promote certain businesses to the public by distributing some promotional materials. If you look around in your everyday life, I'm sure you have came across this type activity in your neighborhood many times without noticing. This can be a piece of paper on the light poll, a flier on your mailbox or a yard signs at a stop light.

ADVANTAGES OF USING PROMOTIONAL ADVERTISING

The question ringing in your mind is, "What are the advantages of using promo ads over media advertising." Here are some of the advantages.

Promotional Advertising can be done on the company's initiative, unlike in the case of media advertising, where the company has to hook up with a media outlet. This can be a hassle if there is no media source nearby or available for taking on the company's advertising demands.

Repetition is the key to success in media advertising. For example, if there's an ad or commercial shown on television, the ad has to be repeatedly shown to make sure that the public will remember the business. On the other hand, Promotional Advertising needs to be done only once. Advertising using promotional items is possible even with a limited budget without devaluing the value of the promotions. In most cases, businesses with inadequate funds may want to use and outsource a promotional company's resources to perform the promotions on their behalf. Most components in media advertising is the company's ability to extend their customer range.

PROMOTIONAL GIFTS BUILD BRAND AWARENESS

Advertising generally entails using a clear, short, and simple message to attract the attention of people. To effectively promote something, you must make sure that you are getting the right attraction and that the brand message you are relaying is coming out as clearly and understandable as possible. Remember, you must stay focused on your target market and its demographics and determine the best way to attract this group of people to your products, services, or business.

It's so important to consider some crucial factors when purchasing promotional or advertising gifts. Utilizing and implementing such items in your marketing plans means that you need to consider the products you choose carefully. Once you select a product, you first need to consider what color you want it to be. This may seem like an unimportant or simple factor, but it has a large impact on the potential of your advertising success. The product's color is the initial thing that will grab your audience's attention. You should try to pick vibrant and bright colors, but if you are going to distribute promotional clothing or apparel, you don't want to have boring or tacky colors or wack clothing designs. Apparel is meant to be worn, and if the color is not what your target market likes to wear, you will end up wasting your money, and your message will not be conveyed or seen by enough people. A lot of companies use promotional advertising gifts to obtain increased recognition of their company's logo or brand. When using these products to enhance logo visibility and recognition, you should try to give something that's useful and practical. Another effective tactic is to consistently use the same product in all your product promotions and advertising. I've found that using humor is another good way to attract consumers to a business. It not only grabs your target market's attention, but it is also great for brightening up someone's day or lifting someone's spirits. When making use of comedy, such as a funny saying or a humorous cartoon or picture, you should make sure that it is something that your target audience will find appealing rather than offensive or repulsive. With some creativity and use of your imagination, you can get some great promotional advertising gifts to promote your business. Follow the tips that you pick up from your current customers, from people around you, and business partners and associates. Combine the knowledge from these people, and you will come up with a good product and a smart advertising and promotional plan.

If you want to browse through or shop from a large selection and variety of items, then hop online and visit different vendors and websites for wholesale items and custom pieces. Remember, businesses that are both big and small can use promotional items as advertising gifts. The reason for this is because the benefits of advertising via such products are time tested and proven. So, if you are searching for the right method for advertising, then definitely consider these items. This approach can have a very positive impact on your brand as well as your company image.

7 BUDGETING YOUR BUSINESS CAPITAL

Getting started with your own business is not as easy as having the money for your initial start up cost and eagerness to earn. You have to think about how you will budget your initial capital so that you don't end up miserable, just in case your business does not turn out as you have planned it. Before you get into earning, you must think about the importance of savings.

One very important business preparations that you must include in your initial capital is for your office building, venue space or store front. Be sure to own or rent an office building that is appropriately designed for your business. Purchasing the materials, equipment, and everything else you need in the construction can be very costly. Many people in business wait until it's too late to understand the value of budgeting. Even though budgets are essential to plan for your company, starting your business is ESSENTIAL BEFORE. Why? You have to decide whether the company/business sales will cover its costs and if it doesn't, the company will collapse before it even begins making money (generating revenue). The business, therefore, has to be able to pay its way for its expenses, or it won't continue. Why that is so important is obvious!

WHAT IS A BUDGET PLAN?

Budgets are used to prepare the costs that the company will require and the profits that the business expects to produce.

In short, as an entrepreneur, you have to:

Comprehend the cash outflow (expenses) and understand the

company's cash inflow (revenue). All entrepreneurs have the same goal which is to be profitable. It also makes sense to put in place a plan for evaluating whether the company will be profitable. To achieve this, a budget will help. Although budget plans can often be seen as terrifying, they are necessary and should not be ignored. The money and numbers are often considered one of a company's driest sections-some would even say boring! It's important to have respect and appreciation for "working with the numbers" in your business, especially if you are a new entrepreneur. Focus on the amount of benefits and information that you can get from budgeting.

IS CREATING A BUDGET PLAN DIFFICULT?

No question about making a budget can be difficult. The level of detail, time, an expectation that can be part of the process of budgeting is always complicated even for those who are well versed in it. Larger companies, states, and non-profit organizations require more complex and includes a tedious budgeting processes. They must create budgets for more than just the owners as they are interested in the company for several interested parties and stakeholders.

With start-up businesses, this is specific in terms of their budget. Small business owners, mainly start-ups, need not to prepare overly, lengthy and comprehensive budgets, or business plans. New companies will have a draft budget plan which will include the start-up's key financial necessities for the first year.

This Preliminary Budget Plan aims to get you there:
- Consider the advantages of producing the first estimate.
- Feeling comfortabe with budgeting.
- Committed to the discipline of running a budget.
- Understanding the power of how budgeting works.
- Put aside your frustration/anxiety about budgeting.

Often, it seems as if everything has been considered, but there may be certain aspects that have not been addressed appropriately from a financial perspective. This may leave you feeling confused and unsure about your entrepreneurial abilities.

WHY IS IT CALLED A PRELIMINARY BUDGET PLAN?

There are several variants and variations of budget plans. You can find similar features and are designed for the same purpose which is to help you decide what the income is supposed to be in the business, the direct costs associated with producing this income, and the anticipated expenses. Creating an excessively comprehensive budget plan can be a lot if you start a new company and are in the start-up process. It's called the "Preliminary Budget Plan" because it's a starting point budget created to get you, the entrepreneur, interested right from the start in the process of creating and making a budget. It's being done in a quick, step-by-step fashion. A Preliminary Budget Plan is also simpler and easier to plan. So the Preliminary Budget Plan basically provides you with a basic layout to get your business up and running.

Here's a few questions that should be addressed when a Preliminary Budget Plan applies:

- Check whether the overall revenue will cover the costs .
- Make smart decisions.
- Test your current market progress.
- Oversee market issues.
- Bring valuable strategic business information .

A Preliminary Budget Plan is presented in a step-by-step process that helps you to organize your thoughts and to WRITE DOWN your plans and keeping track of them. This also provides you with a checklist that can be given to interested parties (e.g., banks, investors, etc.) where or when the need arises.

A PRELIMINARY BUDGET PLAN WILL HELP YOU TO:

- Identify what revenue (sales) the company expects to receive.
- Create how much direct costs and capital the company plans to invest.
- Determine whether items 1 and 2 above will result in profitability for the business. As long as you're an entrepreneur, knowing the money is important.

If you are, you will plan a Preliminary Budget Report.

Characteristic traits of a serious entrepreneur:

- An ambitious entrepreneur who is serious about preparing a new company properly and would like to find out how to draw up a business budget.
- An ambitious entrepreneur who has never written a project plan but wants to know-how.
- An ambitious entrepreneur who is doubtful about a budget proposal but would like to research the process and learn more.
- Any entrepreneur who has heard of the budget plans, but is confused and needs some specific instructions on what to do.

HOW DO I CREAT A SIMPLE BUDGET AS ENTREPRENEUR?

Through the Preliminary Budget Plan process, you will:

- Engage in strategies to help you change your attitude on capital.
- Focus on your business's financial intentions.
- Use a simple, step-by-step process to prepare yourselves.
- Create a preliminary report on the company's budget.
- Get some financial clarity over your company.
- Feel comfortable using the process's "simple elegance."

HOW CAN THE BUDGETING PLAN BE AN ASSET TO THE COMPANY OR THE ENTREPRENEUR?

There are other important benefits that you, "the entrepreneur", get from budgeting. It applies especially to:

- Raising trust.
- Improved ability to take the decision.

- Increased capacity to assess options.
- Improved self-esteem with a more consciousness.
- Improved potential for judgment.

Why? The more you can develop, analyze, and appreciate the money aspects of your company, the more you can manage and make your business all that it can be-it 's all literally within reach!

Remember, these are skills that you will have for the LIFETIME of your business as you will ALWAYS need to consider your business budget.

8 THE IMPORTANCE OF TAXES

Tax planning is very similar to financial planning. It involves taking a closer look at your tax situation from one year to the next. People who have financial investments are always checking with their financial advisors to improve their financial situation. If you're going to check with your financial advisor, you should also check with your tax advisor, and see how your financial investments are going to affect your taxes. Tax planning is not just for those people who invest in finance. Tax planning is for everyone, particularly if you are going through financial changes that could affect your tax situation. Many of those financial adjustments may be purchasing a home, buying or selling a rental property, withdrawing money from a pension plan, or starting a business. Your financial condition could be greatly impacted by some of those financial shifts, as well as others. The best time to check with your accountant is to see how it could affect your taxes before you take on any financial responsibilities or activity. They can analyze your tax situation and tell you what action to take so you don't get caught up in debt because of a lot of money being misused or mishandled. Many times, people call their accountants after financial action. That's like closing the door after the horse has left the barn.

Tax planning is also important especially when it comes to paying your taxes. Many people are under the assumption that they have until April, to pay their income tax. That is not entirely correct. The month of April is only a date when your taxes must be paid in full. The law requires that you pay your taxes as you earn money during the year. For those of you who are paid as employees, you have your taxes withheld from your paychecks. Your employer withholds the income tax from your paycheck, and pays that money to the government throughout the year. However, for those who are self-employed (work for yourselves) or have passive income from investments, you may be required to pay your taxes during the year by making estimated tax payments. Estimated tax payments are quarterly tax payments made throughout the tax year (January through December). The law requires that you estimate your tax liability and pay it as you go during the year. The tax laws also require that you make your payments on April 15th, June 15th, September 15th, and January 15 (of the following year). The tax laws allow you to base your estimate on your prior year's tax. If your income is the same year after year, you can do this with ease. Tax preparation will be carried out throughout the year. This can be accomplished for those of you who are self-employed or have passive investment income, as your income will fluctuate year after year. For those of you who undergo any financial changes which could affect your tax situation during the year, you should consult your accountant or tax advisor. Tax planning is important because it can save you quite a bit of money come tax time.

UNDERSTANDING YOUR TAX LIABILITIES AND KNOWING YOUR POSSIBLE SOLUTIONS

Tax burdens are something to be worried about. It's not ever good to imagine what you will go through if the Internal Revenue Service starts hounding you. It's not a pretty sight to wake up to every day, with a representative from the government knocking at your door or your phone ringing off the hook with tax collectors breathing down your neck. Tax burdens seem to take in more victims each year because most of us do not understand how we became a victim in the first place. Certain legislation may provide for specific tax relief. Unfortunately, most of us don't really know exactly how to utilize them. It's a sad reality that the service is still too complicated for ordinary people to comprehend. Even the most established entrepreneurs still see the IRS as a web of unexplained processes and may get caught up in tax issues. When you look at it, there's no discrimination here because the system affects everyone. So as long as you experience a tax burden, you have to answer for the same. Most businesses retain the services of professional tax advisors or lawyers who would be able to protect the enterprise from the IRS's clutches properly. It's not a problem if you have the money to spare for retainer services, but what if you're getting paid by the hour? In this case, one of the better courses of action is to assess your tax liabilities properly than going over the possible options you can take. These tax issues are usually on a case by case basis. It simply means that there will always be people with less problematic tax issues, which will require minimal assistance. There are also circumstances where the tax liabilities can be difficult to overcome, and you will need the help of a tax expert. There are three kinds of tax debt solutions a person can turn to under current tax laws.

These three solutions are:

1. Offer in Compromise
2. IRS Payment Plan
3. Lump Sum Payment

Among these three, "Offer in Compromise" is the more commonly used method of tax relief. The second solution is generally resorted to in case the "Offer in Compromise" fails. The third option is the least popular. I strongly suggest getting guidance from a professional tax specialist. You can no longer continue to go on in business without going over your tax liabilities first and going over your possible options before taking the matter to a tax specialist for help. Do you want to know more about tax debt solutions? All you have to do is take some time and learn how applying for tax relief should be made. Experienced tax relief experts make it possible for you to put those tax burdens to rest ASAP.

9 BUILDING A SUCCESSFUL TEAM

If you're a leader, at least one or probably multiple teams will be following right behind you. Creating a successful team is a challenge, but you can do some easy things to improve this success significantly. See below a few I've put together from past experience and lessons learned.

BE CLEAR ON THE RESULTS

If you're going to have any chance of building a successful team, you need to start by clarifying the outcome or the outcome you want to achieve. The result needs to be specific and written in a language that everyone can and will understand.

BE CLEAR ABOUT THE SKILLS YOU NEED

An effective team needs the correct combination of skills to achieve the results. For example, a football team needs the right combination of defensive, offensive, and imaginative players. A bomb team is no different. Get focused on the skills that are important to achieve the results you want.

BE CLEAR ABOUT THE ATTRIBUTES THAT ARE NEEDED

Skills are important, but they're just part of what helps you get results. These include fields such as inspiration, shaping, building relationships, personal drive, and resilience, to name but a few. When building your team, make sure you don't lose sight of having the right attributes.

BRING OUT THE BEST IN EVERYONE

To focus on what people aren't good at based on their job title is all too easy. You know, the things people say day after day like advertisers are the only innovative ones, and accountants take no chances, quality control gets in the way, human capital, to name just a few, are all too "rules-based". Make sure you find out what people can bring to the table instead of just guessing or assuming what they can or can't do.

RECOGNIZE THAT IT TAKES TIME

No team ever jumps from forming to performing right away. They are going to go through a series of stages where they are heading forward, turning back, working together, creating friction, and reaching obstacles. Consider that and see it as a short-term loss for a greater gain in the long run. Bottom line is, teams should be able to produce better results. So, what do you need to do as a leader differently to get your team to be more successful?

STEPS TO BUILD A SUCCESSFUL TEAM

Before we continue, it's important to remember that teams exist for one reason: to produce results! It's also important to say that teams need to be sustainable in order to continue delivering positive results. That's why we look at the team members' interrelationships to make sure that all relationships operate at the level the team needs to continue to keep delivering results without burning out. Look at this process of creating a productive team to allow the team to reach the next levels of success and be efficient all while achieving the desired results.

MEASURE THE CURRENT EFFECTIVENESS OF YOUR TEAM

To help the team be more successful, it's important to look at how successful the team is currently. Measuring your team can be a benchmark for team growth, as it offers you an up-to-date evaluation of your team as it operates today. The easiest way is to measure the squad 's effectiveness, which can be achieved in several ways:

- Personal interviews:

Asking each member of the team a clear set of questions designed to assess their success is a great way to learn about what is going on within the team. The disadvantage of this method is that during face-to-face interviews, some of the team members will not be honest and provide transparent information because they are not anonymous. Results are better obtained when you know the feedback is honest.

- Clear measurement:

A very easy way to use this technique is to ask the team members, "How successful is this team on a scale of 1 to 10?", and see what their answers are to encourage you to follow-up with additional questions to learn more about their perceptions of the team and company overall.

- Assessment tool:

The best way to assess the team's current condition confidentially and impartially, is to make members of the team feel confident in the conversation by being trustworthy. This is when they are usually very truthful and transparent with their answers. Instead, the assessment results will be shared with the team as a part of a structured team development plan that involves activities to help the team progress in areas that's needed and necessary.

CREATING A SUCCESS TEAM

This stage is about using your imagination to build the most effective, efficient, and cohesive team you want! Your team's vision could include the following components:

- The principles, goals and expected results for this team.

- Productivity factors:

These are factors that Team Diagnostic International defines as factors that supports the team in achieving results, performing tasks, staying on course to achieve goals and goals. By having qualities like transparency, decision making, setting targets, etc.

- Positivity factors:

Team Diagnostic International describes these as factors that reflect on the interrelationships between team members and the attitude or tone of the team as a group. They include strengths such as confidence, respect, clear communication, conflict management, camaraderie, etc.

I encourage you to start to build your "desired dream team". Schedule a meeting ASAP so that everybody can take part in this innovative process! Recall thinking out of the box — what is it like to have a team that produce outcomes beyond what you think today is possible?

COMMUNICATE EFFECTIVELY

Here's the most important things to keep in mind from my team working experiences:

Everybody receives different details. Some people need to see it, and others need to hear it and so on. Which details do you want to receive? Just because one way works for you, it doesn't work the same way for all of your team members.

Find out and learn how to process information for each person needs to receive. Ask the members of your team, "How do you like to get the information? "They can tell you whether they're visual learners, auditory learners, and so on.

Try to use many different approaches to share crucial information so that all of the team members access the information that you are trying to communicate and deliver.

TURNING YOUR TEAM FROM VISION INTO REALITY

Now that you have learned your team's current effectiveness, you have created a vision of your desired team and you are determined how to best communicate with them, and it's time to create your plan of action!

This move is created to build goals and formulate strategies that will help you develop your team to grow and get to the next levels of success. See below a few of the basics I've put together to help you identify and formulate setting your goals which are:

- Specific
- Measurable
- Attainable
- Realistic
- Time-oriented (Make sure every target has a deadline!)

LEADING YOUR TEAM

Whether you see yourself as your team's "leader," or your team's "leader," or your team's "member," you 're in a position to influence your team. Take a stand to get the squad strengthened! Here are some ways I reccomend you might do this:

- Remind your team members about the dream you have for yourself, your family, your team, most importantly- your business and what you expect from and for your team as much as possible. Remember, they will grow to the next levels and ask them what it takes for them to rise to the next level with you as your business grows.

- Look for ways to build the team and to grow it. When was the last time your manager had a meeting devoted to strengthening the relationships with your colleagues? When was your team's last time to lunch together, or did another fun activity? If you're not familiar with the types of team development techniques that will be effective for your team or don't have the time or expertise to develop a program, call an expert to help you create your team's program.

- Bonuses and incentives can always be fun! Who doesn't enjoy friendly competitive competitions inside the company that allows you to win or make so extra cash?

It's easier than you think to spend time, energy, efforts and financial resources in team building— it doesn't have to be difficult or time-consuming. The crucial thing is that you are consistently do something to keep your team inspired, committed, and efficient to deliver the results you and your company wants and needs to grow!

> "If I dont do it who will?"
>
> JAZMINE CHEAVES

10 ORGANIZING & STAYING CONNECTED WITH YOUR CUSTOMERS

When you're a business owner, keeping your business operations organized is one of the greatest challenges. Especially with new small business ventures, you start your enterprise as a "one-man-show." Meaning, you're the executive, the strategist, the marketer, the receptionist, the order fulfillment manager, the customer relations supervisor, and the maintenance engineer.... and that's just for starters. To operate efficiently and successfully, you have to keep all of these areas organized and controlled. For example, as an internet marketer, you often find out that over time, you have purchased so many software programs that you hardly know what you have, where it is, or what to do with it. Has that ever happened to you? Is your computer filled with various programs you've purchased from a variety of different sources, and intended for purposes you can't quite remember because you don't have all of the information in an easy-to-find system?

Trying to make a way through files and programs whose purpose you don't remember, and from whom or where you purchased can be very time consuming and definitely a "time-waster." Internet marketers are known for purchasing large volumes of digital products as a part of doing business. Research and keeping up with the latest marketing trends, as well as accumulating products for marketing and distribution purposes can be a fundamental part of operations. Not being able to keep track of the products and digital information you've purchased can be a complete disaster for your business.

To organize your digital product collectives, it's best to document and keep track of the following basic information:

- When and where the commodity was bought from.
- What specific rights or licenses were granted with purchase.
- A record of the product features, benefits, sales terms and guarantees.
- Where the product is located on your hard drive.
- Notes regarding the product's purpose or intended use.
- Niche or target market to which the product pertains to.
- Setting up an efficient, easily used, and easily accessible management system for the digital information on your computer is a smart way for you to incorporate time management benefits into your business operations, make your computer files more useful, your business more efficient and profitable.

GENERAL ACCOUNTING SOFTWARE

As a small business owner, you juggle over a dozen of tasks every day. You have to make sure that your employees are providing top customer service. You have to oversee your business' advertising materials. You have to hire the right people, balance your books, and prospect for new business leads and potential customers or clients. It can be a lot for anyone to handle, but you can find help in the form of many apps and softwares created to help you manage all these important things. These apps and softwares can help even the busiest business owners keep track of all of their transactions. Do you track your spending and sales data by hand? Do you keep records of your sales on paper, only to lose half of your information? Nowadays, that's the wrong way to run a company. You need every advantage you can get to keep your business thriving. Many apps and softwares like General Ledger Accounting software lets you create and manage budgets, view a well-organized list of all of your business' accounts, track fixed assets, and monitor all of your business' many transactions. This software stores all of these important data in one place. Now, you can access this information with the touch of a computer key. Some softwares and apps require an upfront investment but think of all the times you will save money in the future. Your talents as the owner of a small business depends on acquiring new clients or customers, creating successful marketing campaigns, and finding the top people to work at your business. Leave the hassle of bookkeeping and accounting to the software or apps designed specifically to handle such chores.

Accounting apps and softwares cab be an easy way to boost your productivity instantly. You need to stop spending your valuable time trying to balance the accounts and allow these powerful accounting software tackle this chore instead. You might be surprised at how much more you get done each day.

KEEP YOUR BUSINESS ORGANIZED TO SAVE TIME AND MONEY

There are so many things involved in running your own business, that being organized is not just a good idea- it's an absolute must! Good organization skills isn't just a matter of keeping your desk clean. You must also be able to find what you need- when you need it, be aware of what is coming up, and move smoothly from one task to the next. To become and stay organized, you will need to develop your organizational system using the tools that work best for you, a calendaring system that is accurate and accessible, and a "to-do' like system that will keep you on track and efficient.

There is no right or wrong way to get or stay organized. Different systems works differently for different people, so there are many different organizational systems, self-help books, and full-time organizational consultants in the market to utilize. If you are like me, you have probably tried one or more of the trendy organizational systems for a certain amount of time and found yourself less committed to it as time goes by. In most cases, this happens because some piece or pieces of the program don't work for you, either because the way it is done doesn't fit your personality, your way of thinking or because your priorities do not align with the design of the organizational system.

The purpose of an organizational system is to help you identify what needs to be done at any given time and plan to accomplish those tasks as efficiently and productively as possible. As a business owner, your organizational system must include a plan with tools for organizing all of the documentation and information required for your business, organizing both your professional as well as your personal life, and for setting an organizational standard for your staff. Even if you are starting by yourself, the habits you set now will have an impact on the culture of your company as you grow.

INTERNAL ORGANIZATIONAL TOOLS

Your business requires sufficient tools to keep all systems and information organized. See below a few bullet point I've put together to highlight this subject topic:

- Paper Filing Systems:

Your Accounting and Contact Management Software can be an excellent tools to provide your organizational foundation, but the paperwork to back up those systems must be logically arranged and accessible. Be sure the system you select is effective for your habits and personality. Organizational systems are only effective if you use it as designed. As your business is up and running, it will be clearer which types of paperwork will be needed most often and only need to be saved.

- Document Options:

For your business documents, you may chose to use hanging files, vertical files, 3-ring binders, or even digital storage. Be sure the system you choose will cover most of your business's priorities. File folders tend to be the default way, although many business owners find them difficult to keep organized. With file folders, the documents are less likely to be correctly ordered, and misfiling is common. It is more difficult to retrieve a specific document from file folders, and they tend to become overfilled quickly. 3-ring binders are effective for keeping a large volume of related materials together and accessible. Digitizing your documents is a space and can be time-efficient, as long as you develop an easy-to-use filing system by creating titled files, folders, and sub-folders to organize the data.

- Accounting Software:

Your accounting system organizes and records all of your business' financial information. It is so important to set up your accounts correctly from the start and record all your business transactions. Checking the books should be on your daily schedule. Depending on your business, you may want to run sales or expense reports, inventory spot checks, or any other accounting task that is most likely to be a problem every day. When you find errors (and you will), it is important to fix them correctly (by finding the balancing error). If you just add or subtract a few dollars each time to make it balance, you will end up with grossly inaccurate financial statements over time. Most softwares will allow you to make changes as needed, but if you don't balance both debit and credit accounts, the extra will go into a separate account reserved for unbalanced amounts. That account will show on your financial statements, and any banker or investor who reviews your reports will want to know why it is there. Your best bet is to fix any and all errors as soon as possible.

- Contact Management Software:

CSM programs are an excellent tool for keeping your customer, vendor, and networking information organized. Keep up with your database by scheduling monthly checks. You can clean your list by ensuring there are no repeated contact entries and marking anyone who has requested to be off your mailing list. It is better to leave those entries in and mark them as unusable rather than deleting them because you will not accidentally re-add them later. Contact management software also helps you keep in touch with your networking contacts by allowing you to enter your last few interactions with each of them. You can sort the list of contacts, see who you need to contact and keep in touch with important contacts in just a few minutes per month.

- Calendar/Planning System:

Select a daily planner that is flexible enough to allow you to customize it to fit your needs. Everyone has multiple priorities including work, family, extracurricular, and it can be very difficult to keep those lives completely separate. Don't assume any particular time-management system should work for you, regardless of how effective they may claim to be. There are a million "right" ways to manage your time, and as long as you create a system that keeps you on track and out of the way- you are good to go. If you have trouble with time-management, look for a customizable calendar system. Check different approaches before you find the one that works best for you, and then use it!

Using a calendaring system is an absolute must for small business owners. There are so many different aspects to keep up with and so many dates and deadlines to remember that they must be written down and effectively organized to keep any entrepreneur on track. Avoid selecting an undersized planner. Most entrepreneurs ultimately agree that a full-size (81/2 x 11) time-management system ends up like an extra appendage - they don't leave home without it. A planner in a 3-ring notebook is great for a startup, as you can keep the various papers organized when you are on the go. Whatever tools you choose to keep you and your business organized, make sure they work for you and fit with your intended culture. Don't hesitate to make changes if any part isn't working -- the cost of organizational tools will more than pay for themselves in the time they will save. Be sure to establish effective organizational and time-management systems and be diligent about using them.

The three tools every entrepreneur should have are

1. A filing system for paper documents.
2. A calendaring system.
3. A contact management software.

Be aware of the way you spend your time. Spend a couple of minutes analyzing your day every morning, night, and planning the next. Try not to burn yourself out and remember, entrepreneurship is a marathon, not a sprint!

STAYING CONNECTED WITH YOUR CUSTOMERS

In this day in age where cell phone devices are a prominent feature of society, businesses can now connect with customers through a wider range in so many ways. If you're looking for a fresh and innovative approach that will keep your customers engaged with your business, mobile marketing is definitely the solution. One of the most effective things about mobile marketing is the use of mobile applications (also known as apps). To develop an effective application, it would be worth seeking a technical expert's advice to assist you. A mobile application can be offered to customers to simplify doing business with your company. Mobile applications provide an unlimited level of connections between companies and customers. Customers who download a company's mobile apps are then able to connect with that company through other platforms, such as social media or directly through the company's website. An appealing mobile application has the potential to encourage about 80% of people to download it within an hour. Very few marketing materials or tools can establish such a connection with a target audience like mobile apps.

MOBILE APPLICATION MARKETING PLAN

Once your business has developed an engaging and interactive mobile application, the next step is to consider how to promote your business. For example, a 'fun' application could be she was used as a gift, which will act as an incentive to drive traffic to your website. A 'functional' application (i.e., something that requires a response, such as filling out a form) can allow customers to establish a connection with your business as well as encourage them to use the service your business has to offer. Why not consider offering your mobile app free of charge? Offering a free app that drives traffic to your website to download it will not only increase your search engine page rank, but the increased volume of people visiting your site will also raise public awareness from your site and your business, which can eventually turn in to an increase in company sales and revenue.

Aside from apps, a large number of mobile devices and different platforms are now available to people. Meaning that connecting with customers can be achieved in so many ways. Mobile phones, smartphones, and iPhones offer marketing through SMS, e-mail, and social networking. Other advances in technology such as the Apple iPad and the Kindle means mobile marketing can be achieved on a global scale. Marketing through mobile devices is considered to be 'the future' of marketing and advertising as they do offer constant connectivity with consumers or customers that are constantly on the move. I definitely suggest you get with the program and join the future of marketing.

DIRECT EMAIL MARKETING

What could be more frustrating than getting someone to your website and then seeing them leave? Direct mail marketing is the definitely the solution to this problem. It removes the possibility of the lost customer and most importantly, losing the sale. It may take many different marketing strategies before a customer actually trusts you enough to make a purchase. Adding a signup box to your website and collecting the site's visitors' email address can never be a bad idea. Getting the person's permission to contact them and create a stylish email marketing promotion to get them back to your site creates a revolving door that only bring them back to your site where they feel special because of your exclusive products, deals and a few promotional offers. This will have them drooling over your ads, and there will be a boost in the traffic as well as sales. To achieve these benefits, you must do a thorough check on your customer's desires, wants, and expectations and make an offer no one can refuse. The more you target your email marketing message, the greater your response rate will be and the faster people will come back to your online store or website to place orders. The goal is always to outdo the competition in every way possible and with direct email marketing campaigns, you can definately get your store information and special offers in their inbox. It should be done so effectively that when that purchase time comes, your product should sell out like hotcakes. Direct email marketing is a meant to build relationships with your customers while making them want to buy from you each and every time. By staying connected with your customers, you will develop an edge over the others because your offers will extend beyond your website and into the inbox of potential buyers.

> "Turn that hurt into some hustle!"
>
> — JAZMINE CHEAVES

ABOUT THE AUTHOR

JAZMINE "AMEERAH" CHEAVES

Jazmine Ameerah Cheaves, popularly known as "Lookin Ameerah", or simply referred to as "Bigg Jazz", is a serial entrepreneur, social media influencer and published author who hails from the southern city of Savannah, Georgia.

Born on September 26, 1995, this dynamic young powerhouse now resides in Atlanta, and is the founder of the well established beauty brand,

The Glam Trap.

She also has her own luxury line of dinnerware, pots and cooking products named "Lookin Ameerah Cookware".

She is also a top selling author of her books "Entrepreneurship Talk with a Real Ass Boss!" #1 Handbook Guide and her cooking guide entitled "Lookin A Cookbook" both released in 2020.

Just a few short years ago, no one, including Jazmine, expected that she would become an accomplished business mogul that would earn millions by the age of 25.

Interestingly enough, she was a mischievous child, but an exceptional student who attended private schools in Savannah all the way until college. She was accepted to Georgia State University where she would later graduate with a degree in adolescent psychology. Her life had all of the makings of a traditional hardworking professional with a good 9 to 5 job. However, after taking a closer look at her background, it's clear that entrepreneurship and innovation was in her blood.

Jazmine's Stepfather, who she lived with for most of her life, along with her mother and siblings, owned an underground surveying company for the government. Through him, she was able to observe the hard work, dedication and attention to detail that was required to own and operate a business. On her biological father's side of the family, which she refers to as her "hood side," she developed street smarts, an understanding of popular culture and the ability to identify trends in lifestyle and fashion.

While at Georgia State, Jazmine's parents did not want her to work, preferring her to focus entirely on her studies. Still, she insisted that she needed something to keep her stimulated and to give her a sense of independence. She decided to sign up for lash classes, and that move would soon change her life forever.

Once she learned the trade and became certified, Jazmine did lashes for girls in her college dorm room, and from her mother's sofa when she was at home from school.

Deciding that she would have to create her own opportunity, in 2014, while still making the Dean's List in college, Jazmine casted fear aside and launched her first business, officially introducing The Glam Trap. Her parents had no idea she had ventured into entrepreneurship until she surprised them with the keys to her new shop.

Not long after, Jazmine began teaching lash classes of her own, and in no time, catapulted to success and relevance. In fact, at her very first class, she registered 80 participants and made a whopping $50,000 in one day!

She then organized her own lash tours, taking her classes to cities around the country, amassing a large fan-base in the process, and making 10's of thousands of dollars each outing.

Jazmine currently has a following of almost 400,000 across her Instagram accounts and she has been featured in numerous media outlets. The Glam Trap studio is big business, offering an array of items or customer including high-end lash extensions, quality wigs, cosmetic products and apparel.

For her followers and supporters, Jazmine shares her passions of cooking, fashion and creating the next big thing. She also aims to inspire them to always think big and to never doubt themselves.

After all, her rejection from others is what opened the doors for a life she never could have imagined.

Favorite Quotes:

- "If you have a plan, go with it."
- "It doesn't matter if people believe in you, you can make them a believer."

To learn more about Jazmine Cheaves, visit:

RealAssBoss.com

Made in the USA
Columbia, SC
05 September 2020